The WISDOM
of the SAINTS

BLUE SPARROW
North Palm Beach, Florida

BLUE
sparrow

Copyright © 2022
Kakadu, LLC
Published by BLUE SPARROW

The quotes in this book have been drawn from dozens of sources.
They are assumed to be accurate as quoted in their previously
published forms. Although every effort has been made to verify the
quotes and sources, the Publisher cannot guarantee their perfect
accuracy.

Cover Art:
Communion of Saints
Used with Permission, Copyright 2003
John Nava/The Cathedral of Our Lady of the Angels

ISBN: 978-1-63582-192-5 (hardcover)
ISBN: 978-1-63582-193-2 (e-Book)

10   9   8   7   6   5   4   3   2   1

Printed in the United States of America

FIRST EDITION

INTRODUCTION:

SOONER OR LATER, we all rise or fall to the level of our friendships. It's a simple, but life-altering truth. The people we surround ourselves with either raise or lower our standards. They either help us to become the-best-version-of-ourselves or encourage us to become lesser versions of ourselves. We become like our friends.

The book you are holding in your hands is an invitation to become friends with some of the greatest men and women who have ever lived. In these pages you will encounter the voices of the saints, their greatest insights into how to live well, their most inspiring wisdom for growing in virtue, and their most powerful advice for stepping into the heart of God.

In order to fully embrace that experience, we first need to acknowledge a major obstacle to truly knowing the saints and accepting their wisdom. Far too often we view the saints as unapproachable in their holiness. We think they are not like us or that it is impossible for us to live the way they lived. We actually dehumanize them by placing them on pedestals and stripping away the reality of who they were as human beings. We minimize their own struggles to follow God's will. And we forget that the virtues they practiced and the wisdom they gained were developed in the ordinary moments of day-to-day life.

How can we rediscover the beautiful humanity of the saints? By walking and talking with them and allowing them to speak directly into our lives. Then, we can see the saints for who they really are: Not unrealistic examples of holiness, but our greatest companions and friends in our own struggle to find joy and make sense of life. And by discovering their beautiful humanity, we will discover our own.

As you get to know the saints on a more personal level, one of the most beautiful things you will experience is their rich diversity. Every saint was a unique human being with their own distinct personality. Each of them related to God in a special and powerful way. And each walked their own particular path of holiness. St. Teresa of Calcutta served at the bedside of the dying and neglected. Thomas Aquinas contemplated the nature of God in his study. Peter walked with Jesus and became the rock of the Church. Thérèse of Lisieux found God in the little acts of ordinary life. And the list goes on. There is an almost endless litany of examples that can help animate our lives.

Saints represent every race, come from every culture, and span the centuries. Male and female, young and old, rich and poor, introverted and extroverted, practical and mystical, the saints are a kaleidoscope of the human experience. There is literally no aspect of life that the collection of saints has not experienced, no emotion they have not felt, no doubt they have not faced, no suffering they have not endured. And so, wherever you are on your spiritual journey, whether you are young or old, whatever your personality and unique talents may be, and whatever may have happened in your past, the saints can offer you the encouragement and friendship you yearn for here and now.

One of the incredible gifts the saints give us as we encounter the many experiences of life is the breadth and depth of their own collective experiences. Everything you will ever experience has been experienced by a saint. Everything.

But perhaps the greatest legacy of the saints is that they have not left us to discover the keys to the good life on our own or from scratch. Physically, emotionally, intellectually, and especially spiritually, the saints have gone ahead and mapped the path to deeper fulfillment and happiness for us. And now, in the words that follow, they offer you the most essential wisdom you will need for your own journey.

How will becoming friends with the saints change your life? In many ways, the answer will be deeply personal for you. The saints will bring you the surprising, relevant, and transformative wisdom you need to become perfectly yourself. It will be an experience as beautiful and unique as you are. But there is one way a friendship with the saints changes us all, no matter who we are or where we come from.

A friendship with the saints always leads us to a friendship with God. This is the mark of all great friendships and every saint offers it to us fully. In the staggering variety of the saints, we find that what unites them all is that each of them spent their lives drawing close to God. The saints know God in the intimate ways we yearn to know Him. They are wrapped up in His love and want to draw us into that experience. Accept their invitation and your life will never be the same again.

No man becomes great on his own. No woman becomes great on

her own. We all need people in our lives who inspire us, show us what is possible, raise our standards, remind us of our essential purpose, and challenge us to become the-best-version-of-ourselves. It is my hope that this book helps you to step into a new and ever-deepening friendship with the saints so that you may know, love, and serve God like never before.

— MATTHEW KELLY

JANUARY

January 1 _____ *Trusting God*

"Be who God meant you to be and you will set the world on fire."

– St. Catherine of Siena

January 2 _____ *Life*

"Pray as though everything depended on God. Work as though everything depended on you."

– St. Augustine

January 3 _____ *Sadness*

"Earth has no sorrow that heaven cannot heal."

– St. Thomas More

January 4 _____ *Life*

"Live simply so that others may simply live."

– St. Elizabeth Ann Seton

January 5 ———————— *Redemption*

"It is not he who begins well who is perfect. It is he who ends well who is approved in God's sight."

– St. Basil the Great

January 6 ———————— *Prayer*

"A man of prayer is capable of everything."

– St. Vincent de Paul

January 7 ———————— *Mercy*

"Mercy is the greatest attribute of God."

– St. Faustina

January 8 ———————— *Joy*

"The soul of one who serves God always swims in joy, always keeps holiday, and is always in the mood for singing."

– St. John of the Cross

January 9 —————————— *Trust in God*

"Nothing can happen to me that God doesn't want. And all that He wants, no matter how bad it may appear to us, is really for the best."

– St. Thomas More

January 10 —————————— *Friendship*

"God sends us friends to be our firm support in the whirlpool of struggle. In the company of friends, we will find strength to attain our sublime ideal."

– St. Maximilian Kolbe

January 11 —————————— *Femininity*

"You, who have the kingdom of heaven, are not a poor little woman, but a queen."

– St. Jordan of Saxony

January 12 —————————— *Parenting*

"If you want to bring happiness to the whole world, go home and love your family."

– St. Teresa of Calcutta

January 13 —————————— *Work*

"The first end I propose in our daily work is to do the will of God; secondly, to do it in the manner he wills it; and thirdly to do it because it is his will."

– St. Elizabeth Ann Seton

January 14 —————————— *Marriage*

"It takes three to make love, not two: you, your spouse, and God. Without God people only succeed in bringing out the worst in one another. Lovers who have nothing else to do but love each other soon find there is nothing else. Without a central loyalty life is unfinished."

–Bl. Fulton Sheen

January 15 —————————— *True Strength*

"Learn to be stronger in spirit than in your muscles. If you are, you will be real apostles of faith in God."

– Bl. Pier Giorgio Frassati

January 16 —————————— *Wealth*

"Your wealth is measured by the lack of your needs, not by the abundance of your possessions."

– St. Charbel Makhlouf

January 17 ——————————— *Sacrifice*

"Good is never accomplished except at the cost of those who do it, truth never breaks through except through the sacrifice of those who spread it."

– St. John Henry Newman

January 18 ——————————— *True Greatness*

"You aspire to great things? Begin with little ones."

– St. Benedict

January 19 ——————————— *Society*

"Disorder in society is the result of disorder in the family."

– St. Angela Merici

January 20 ——————————— *Our Crosses in Life*

Quote: "There is no cross to bear that Christ has not already born for us, and does not now bear with us."

– St. John Paul the Great

January 21 ——————— *Holy Scripture*

"Be constantly committed to prayer or to reading Scripture; by praying, you speak to God, in reading, God speaks to you."

– St. Cyprian of Carthage

January 22 ——————— *Suffering*

"If God causes you to suffer much, it is a sign that He has great designs for you, and that He certainly intends to make you a saint."

– St. Ignatius of Loyola

January 23 ——————— *Patience*

"The fruits of the earth are not brought to perfection immediately, but by time, rain and care; similarly, the fruits of men ripen through ascetic practice, study, time, perseverance, self-control and patience."

– St. Anthony the Great

January 24 ——————— *Trust in God*

"Who gives you the day will give you also the things necessary for the day."

– St. Gregory of Nyssa

January 25 —————————— *The Cross*

"Whenever you are given a cross, be sure to embrace it with humility and gratitude. If God, in His infinite goodness, favors you with a cross of some importance, be sure to thank him in a special way"

– St. Louis de Montfort

January 26 —————————— *Prayer*

"The greater and more persistent your confidence in God, the more abundantly you will receive all that you ask."

– St. Albert the Great

January 27 —————————— *Grace*

"Grace comes after tribulation."

– St. Rose of Lima

January 28 —————————— *Virtue*

"We can never know how patient or humble someone is when everything is going well with him. But when those who should cooperate with him do exactly the opposite, then we can know. A man has as much patience and humility as he has then, and no more."

– St. Francis of Assisi

January 29 ——————— *Happiness*

"The secret of happiness is to live moment by moment and to thank God for all that He, in His goodness, sends to us day after day."

– St. Giana Molla

January 30 ——————— *Disappointment*

"If disappointed, don't say hard things. Only think a little, pray a little, and try to remember that God will bring about what is best in God's own time."

– St. Mary MacKillop

January 31 ——————— *Material Possessions*

"Aspire not to have more, but to be more."

– St. Oscar Romero

FEBRUARY

February 1 —————————— *Courage*

"Go forward bravely. Fear nothing. Trust in God; all will be well."

— *St. Joan of Arc*

February 2 —————————— *Truth*

"Speak the truth in a million voices. It is silence that kills."

— *St. Catherine of Siena*

February 3 —————————— *Love of Neighbor*

"Every human being is neighbor to every other human being. Is this person known as a friend? Let them stay as a friend. Is this person your enemy? Let them become a friend."

— *St. Augustine*

February 4 —————————— *Evangelization*

"Actions speak louder than words; let your words teach and your actions speak."

— *St. Anthony of Padua*

February 5 ———————————— *Friendship*

"Fly from bad companions as from the bite of a poisonous snake. If you keep good companions, I can assure you that you will one day rejoice with the blessed in Heaven; whereas if you keep with those who are bad, you will become bad yourself, and you will be in danger of losing your soul."

– St. John Bosco

February 6 ———————————— *Happiness*

"I need nothing in this world in order to be happy. I only need to see Jesus in Heaven, Whom I now see and adore on the Altar with the eyes of faith."

– St. Dominic Savio

February 7 ———————————— *Study*

"Never begin or end your study but by prayer."

– St. Vincent Ferrer

February 8 ———————————— *Joy*

"A word or a smile is often enough to put fresh life in a despondent soul."

– St. Therese of Lisieux

February 9 —————————————— *Faith*

"Great occasions for serving God come seldom, but little ones surround us daily."

— *St. Francis de Sales*

February 10 ————————— *God's Mercy*

"There is no saint without a past, no sinner without a future."

— *St. Augustine*

February 11 ————————————— *Work*

"He who labors as he prays lifts his heart to God with his hands."

— *St. Benedict*

February 12 ——————— *Masculinity*

"It is almost a definition of a gentleman to say that he is one who never inflicts pain."

— *St. John Henry Newman*

February 13 —————— *Thanksgiving*

"Attribute to God every good that you have received. If you take credit for something that does not belong to you, you will be guilty of theft."

– St. Anthony of Padua

February 14 —————— *Relationships*

"When a young man or woman recognizes that authentic love is a precious treasure, they are also enabled to live their sexuality in accordance with the divine plan, rejecting the false models which are, unfortunately, all too frequently publicized and very widespread."

– St. John Paul the Great

February 15 —————— *Success*

"Luck is when an opportunity comes along and you've prepared for it."

– St. Patrick

February 16 —————— *Helping Others*

"It can only be disgraceful for some Christians to snore while other Christians are in peril."

– St. Thomas More

February 17 ——————————— *Abstinence*

"Abstinence is the mother of health. A few ounces of going without is an excellent recipe for any ailment."

– Bl. Anthony Grassi

February 18 ——————————— *Holiness*

"A servant is not holy if she is not busy."

– St. Zita

February 19 ——————————— *Sports*

"A saint was once asked, while playing happily with his companions, what he would do if an angel told him that in a quarter of an hour he would die and have to appear before the judgment seat of God. The saint promptly replied that he would continue playing because he was certain these games were pleasing to God."

– St. John Bosco

February 20 _____ *Holiness*

"You cannot be half a saint; you must be a whole saint or no saint at all."

– St. Therese of Lisieux

February 21 _____ *Material Possessions*

"I was born poor, I have lived poor, I wish to die poor."

– St. Pope Pius X

February 22 _____ *Our Crosses in Life*

"Crosses release us from this world, and by doing so, bind us to God."

– St. Charles de Foucauld

February 23 _____ *Prayer*

"The success of your morning meditation will largely depend on what you have eaten the night before."

– St. Alphonsus Liguori

February 24 —————————— *Forgiveness*

"Resentment is like drinking poison and waiting for the other person to die."

– St. Augustine

February 25 —————————— *Penance*

"You should be content to do as He wishes, for He is satisfied with far less than you owe Him."

– Bl. Sebastian Valfre

February 26 —————————— *Love Your Enemies*

"We must show love for those who do evil to us and pray for them. Nothing is dearer or more pleasing to God than this."

– St. Bridget of Sweden

February 27 —————————— *God's Will for Us*

"Christian, remember your dignity!"

– St. Pope Leo the Great

February 28 _____ *Peace in Christ*

"Let nothing disturb you, nothing frighten you; all things are passing; God never changes."

– St. Teresa of Avila

February 29 _____ *Happiness*

"Find happiness in making others happy."

– St. Mary MacKillop

MARCH

March 1 _____ *Prayer*

"Every day, when your heart especially feels the loneliness of life, pray."

– St. Padre Pio

March 2 _____ *Love*

"We are born to love, we live to love, and we will die to love still more."

– St. Joseph Cafasso

March 3 _____ *Happiness*

"I have my room, some books, and a nearby chapel. That is complete happiness."

– St. Miguel of Ecuador

March 4 _____ *Love*

"Nothing is more beautiful than love. Indeed, faith and hope will end when we die, whereas love, that is, charity, will last for eternity; if anything, I think it will be even more alive in the next life!"

– Bl. Pier Giorgio Frassati

March 5 _____ *Trusting God*

"I asked you and you would not listen; so I asked my God and He did listen."

— *St. Scholastica*

March 6 _____ *Order*

"External disorder and untidiness are signs of internal disorder."

— *St. Francis de Sales*

March 7 _____ *The Poor*

"Go to the poor: you will find God."

— *St. Vincent de Paul*

March 8 _____ *Faith*

"Start by doing what's necessary; then do what's possible; and suddenly you are doing the impossible."

— *St. Francis of Assisi*

March 9 _____ *Faith*

"Not the goods of the world, but God. Not riches, but God. Not honors, but God. Not distinction, but God. Not dignities, but God. Not advancement, but God. God always and in everything."

– St. Vincent Pallotti

March 10 _____ *Sacrifice*

"Miss no single opportunity of making some small sacrifice, here by a smiling look, there by a kindly word; always doing the smallest right and doing it all for love."

– St. Therese of Lisieux

March 11 _____ *Intimacy with God*

"As all men are touched by God's love, so all are also touched by the desire for His intimacy. No one escapes this longing; we are all kings in exile, miserable without the Infinite."

– Bl. Fulton Sheen

March 12 ———— *Femininity*

"Each woman who lives in the light of eternity can fulfill her vocation, no matter if it is in marriage, in a religious order, or in a worldly profession."

– St. Edith Stein

March 13 ———— *Parenting*

"If I had to advise parents, I should tell them to take great care about the people with whom their children associate... Much harm may result from bad company, and we are inclined by nature to follow what is worse than what is better."

– St. Elizabeth Ann Seton

March 14 ———— *Society and Culture*

"You are surprised that the world is losing its grip? That the world is grown old? Don't hold onto the old man, the world; don't refuse to regain your youth in Christ, who says to you: 'The world is passing away; the world is losing its grip; the world is short of breath. Don't fear, your youth shall be renewed as an eagle.'"

– St. Augustine

March 15 _____ *Relationships*

"As you seek a virtuous spouse, it is fitting that you should be the same."

– St. Bernardino

March 16 _____ *Teaching*

"Better to instruct a child than to collect riches."

– St. Herve of Brittany

March 17 _____ *Evangelization*

"To convert somebody go and take them by the hand and guide them."

– St. Thomas Aquinas

March 18 _____ *True Success*

"Success in life consists of standing without shame before God."

– St. Charbel Makhlouf

March 19 —————————— *Order*

"If your books are in order, your life will be too."
– St. Raymund of Penyafort

March 20 —————————— *Society*

"Today's society does not pray. That is why it is falling apart."
– St. Padre Pio

March 21 —————— *Love of Neighbor*

"If you are angry at your neighbor, you are angry at God…
Honor your neighbor and you have honored God."
– St. Ephrem the Syrian

March 22 ————— *Jesus' Sufferings*

"How could I bear a crown of gold when the Lord bears a
crown of thorns and bears it for me?!"
– St. Elizabeth of Hungary

March 23 ———— *Earthly Treasures*

"It is not a sin to have riches, but to fix our hearts upon them."
– St. Jean Baptiste de la Salle

March 24 ——————— *The Rosary*

"Even if you are on the brink of damnation, even if you have one foot in hell, even if you have sold your soul to the devil as sorcerers do who practice black magic, and even if you are a heretic as obstinate as a devil, sooner or later you will be converted and will amend your life and will save your soul, if–and mark well what I say–if you say the Holy Rosary devoutly every day until death for the purpose of knowing the truth and obtaining contrition and pardon for your sins."

– St. Louis de Montfort

March 25 ——————— *Temptation*

"When tempted, invoke your Angel. He is more eager to help you than you are to be helped! Ignore the devil and do not be afraid of him: He trembles and flees at the sight of your Guardian Angel."

– St. John Bosco

March 26 ——————— *Tribulations*

"Without the struggle of afflictions, It is impossible to reach the height of grace. The gift of grace increases as the struggles increases."

– St. Rose of Lima

March 27 _____ *Desolation*

"In times of desolation you should never make a change, but stand firm in the resolutions and decisions that guided you the day before the desolation."

– St. Ignatius of Loyola

March 28 _____ *Humility*

"Whatever you do, think not of yourself, but of God."

– St. Vincent Ferrer

March 29 _____ *Community*

"When you see a brother, you see God."

– St. Clement of Alexandria

March 30 _____ *Intimacy with God*

"Withdraw often into the depths of your being, and there with living faith rest on the breast of God, like a child, in the sacred silence of faith and holy love."

– St. Paul of the Cross

March 31 _____ *Joy*

"For Christ the Lord is risen. Our joy that hath no end."
                                    – *St. John of Damascus*

APRIL

April 1 _____ *Love*

"You learn to speak by speaking, to study by studying, to run by running, to work by working, and just so, you learn to love by loving. All those who think to learn in any other way deceive themselves."

– St. Francis de Sales

April 2 _____ *Good Thoughts*

"Occupy your mind with good thoughts, or the enemy will fill them with bad ones."

– St. Thomas More

April 3 _____ *Priorities*

"The things that we love tell us what we are."

– St. Thomas Aquinas

April 4 _____ *Friendship*

"A friend is long sought, hardly found, and with difficulty kept."

– St. Jerome

April 5 —————————— *Serving Others*

"Nothing seems tiresome or painful when you are working for a Master who pays well; who rewards even a cup of
cold water given for love of Him."

– St. Dominic Savio

April 6 —————————— *Evangelization*

"We must sow the seed, not hoard it."

– St. Dominic

April 7 —————————— *Hope*

"Your accumulated offences do not surpass the multitude
of God's mercies: your wounds do not surpass the great
Physician's skill."

– St. Cyril of Jerusalem

April 8 —————————— *Knowing God*

"That you may be able to know God, first know yourself."
– St. Cyprian of Carthage

April 9 _____ *Trust in God*

"Cast yourself into the arms of God and be very sure that if He wants anything of you, He will fit you for the work and give you strength."

– St. Philip Neri

April 10 _____ *Reading*

"Read some chapter of a devout book. God speaks to you when you read."

– St. Vincent de Paul

April 11 _____ *Work*

"Without work, it is impossible to have fun."

– St. Thomas Aquinas

April 12 _____ *Opportunity*

"He who loses an opportunity is like the man who lets a bird fly from his hand, for he will never recover it."

– St. John of the Cross

April 13 _____ *The Church*

"The Church is like a great ship being pounded by the waves of life's different stresses. Our duty is not to abandon ship, but to keep her on her course."

– St. Boniface of Mainz

April 14 _____ *Justice*

"The source of justice is not vengeance but charity."

– St. Bridget of Sweden

April 15 _____ *God's Creation*

"You shall find a fuller satisfaction in the woods than in books. The trees and the rocks will teach you what you cannot hear from the masters."

– St. Bernard of Clairvaux

April 16 _____ *Teaching*

"What is nobler than to rule minds or to mold the character of the young?"

– St. John Chrysostom

April 17 ———————————— *Death*

"For I trust, in whatever manner I die, that I shall not be deprived of the mercy of my God."

– St. Gertrude

April 18 ———————————— *Change*

"Nothing great is ever achieved without enduring much.

– St. Catherine of Siena

April 19 ———————————— *Traditions*

"When I go to Rome, I fast on Saturday, but in Milan I do not. Do you also follow the custom of whatever church you attend, if you do not want to give or receive scandal."

– St. Ambrose of Milan

April 20 ———————————— *True Poverty*

"We think sometimes that poverty is only being hungry, naked and homeless. The poverty of being unwanted, unloved and uncared for is the greatest poverty. We must start in our own homes to remedy this kind of poverty."

– St. Teresa of Calcutta

April 21 ———————————— *Suffering*

"Suffering is a great grace; through suffering the soul becomes like the Savior; in suffering love becomes crystallized; the greater the suffering, the purer the love."

– St. Faustina

April 22 ———————————— *Silence*

"Silence is a gift of God, to let us speak more intimately with Him."

– St. Vincent Pallotti

April 23 ———————————— *Resurrection*

"Let us not forget that Jesus not only suffered, but also rose in glory; so, too, we go to the glory of the Resurrection by way of suffering and the Cross."

– St. Maximillian Kolbe

April 24 ———————————— *Generosity*

"Be generous to the poor orphans and those in need. The man to whom our Lord has been liberal ought not to be stingy. We shall one day find in Heaven as much rest and joy as we ourselves have dispensed in this life."

– St. Ignatius of Loyola

April 25 ——————— *Our Crosses in Life*

"The Cross will not crush you; if its weight makes you stagger, its power will also sustain you."

– St. Padre Pio

April 26 ————————————— *Life*

"Live so as not to fear death. For those who live well in the world, death is not frightening but sweet and precious."

– St. Rose of Viterbo

April 27 ——————— *Trusting God*

"Hold your eyes on God and leave the doing to Him. That is all the doing you have to worry about."

– St. Jane Frances de Chantal

April 28 ———————————— *Prayer*

"Prayer is nothing else than being on terms of friendship with God."

– St. Teresa of Avila

April 29 ———————————— *Love*

"I shall love You, I shall love You always; when day breaks, when evening turns into night, at every hour, at every moment; I shall love You always, always, always."

— *St. Gemma Galgani*

April 30 ———————————— *Heaven*

"Jesus told me, 'My heaven would not be complete without you.'"

— *St. Gertrude the Great*

MAY

May 1 ——————— *Feeding the Hungry*

"If you can't feed a hundred people, then feed just one."
– St. Teresa of Calcutta

May 2 ——————————— *Busyness*

"We cannot do everything, and there is a sense of liberation in realizing that."
– St. Oscar Romero

May 3 ——————————— *Bad Times*

"There are no times so bad that a good man cannot live in them."
– St. Thomas More

May 4 ——————————— *Life*

"The best way to prepare for death is to spend every day of life as though it were the last."
– St. Philip Neri

May 5 ————————————— *Change*

"To live is to change, and to be perfect is to have changed often."

– St. John Henry Newman

May 6 ————————————— *Prayer*

"Everything, even sweeping, scraping vegetables, weeding a garden and waiting on the sick could be a prayer, if it were offered to God."

– St. Martin de Porres

May 7 ————————— *Personal Development*

"Good, better, best. Never let it rest. 'til your good is better and your better is best."

– St. Jerome

May 8 ————————————— *Life of Faith*

"God did not tell us to follow Him because He needed our help, but because He knew that loving Him would make us whole."

– St. Irenaeus

May 9 _____ *Love*

"What we love we shall grow to resemble."

– St. Bernard

May 10 _____ *Good Works*

"He who does a pure and whole work for God merits a whole kingdom."

– St. John of the Cross

May 11 _____ *Family Life*

"The family that prays together, stays together, and if they stay together they will love one another as God has loved each one of them. And works of love are always works of peace."

– St. Teresa of Calcutta

May 12 _____ *Health*

"I travel, work, suffer my weak health, meet with a thousand difficulties, but all these are nothing, for this world is so small. To me, space is an imperceptible object, as I am accustomed to dwell in eternity."

– St. Frances Xavier Cabrini

May 13 _____ *Relationships*

"When a man loves a woman, he has to become worthy of her. The higher her virtue, the more noble her character, the more devoted she is to truth, justice, goodness, the more a man has to aspire to be worthy of her. The history of civilization could actually be written in terms of the level of its women."

– Bl. Fulton Sheen

May 14 _____ *Obedience*

"He that is truly obedient does not wait for a command, but as soon as he knows what his superior wishes to have done immediately sets himself to work, without expecting an order."

– St. Albert the Great

May 15 _____ *Sports*

"Sport, properly directed, develops character, makes a man courageous, a generous loser, and a gracious victor."

– St. Pope Pius X

May 16 _____ *Death*

"The business of the Christian is nothing else than to be ever preparing for death."

– St. Irenaeus

May 17 _____ *Generosity*

"Take care of your health, that it may serve you to serve God."

– St. Francis de Sales

May 18 _____ *Evangelization*

"Many, many people hereabouts are not becoming Christians for one reason only: there is nobody to make them Christians."

– St. Francis Xavier

May 19 _____ *Mercy*

"Let no one doubt concerning the goodness of God; even if a person's sins were as dark as night, God's mercy is stronger than our misery."

– St. Faustina

May 20 _____ *The Eucharist*

"The Eucharist is a fire which inflames us."
— *St. John of Damascus*

May 21 _____ *Our Crosses in Life*

"Christians must lean on the Cross of Christ just as travelers lean on a staff when they begin a long journey."
— *St. Anthony of Padua*

May 22 _____ *Our Lady*

"One day, through the Rosary and the Scapular, Our Lady will save the world."
— *St. Dominic*

May 23 _____ *Good Works*

"I know well that the greater and more beautiful the work is, the more terrible will be the storms that rage against it."
— *St. Faustina*

May 24 _____ *Prayer*

"Take even bread with moderation, lest an overloaded stomach make you weary of prayer."

– *St. Bernard of Clairvaux*

May 25 _____ *Temptations*

"To those who are just and upright, temptations become helps."

– *St. Ephrem the Syrian*

May 26 _____ *Generosity*

"Men lose all the material things they leave behind them in this world, but they carry with them the reward of their charity and the alms they give. For these, they will receive from the Lord the reward and recompense they deserve."

– *St. Francis of Assisi*

May 27 _____ *Idleness*

"Idleness is the enemy of the soul."

– *St. Benedict*

May 28 ———————————— *Suffering*

"If there be a true way that leads to the Everlasting Kingdom, it is most certainly that of suffering, patiently endured."

– St. Colette

May 29 ———————————— *Patience*

"Patience is the root and guardian of all the virtues."

– St. Pope Gregory the Great

May 30 ———————————— *Happiness*

"Happiness is to be found only in the home where God is loved and honored, where each one loves, and helps, and cares for the others."

– Bl. Theophane Venard

May 31 ———————————— *Worry*

"Pray, hope, and don't worry. Worry is useless. God is merciful and will hear your prayers."

– St. Padre Pio

JUNE

June 1 ───────────────── *Love*

"Spread love everywhere you go. Let no one ever come to you without leaving happier."

— *St. Teresa of Calcutta*

June 2 ───────────── *Right and Wrong*

"Right is right if no one's doing it; wrong is wrong even if everyone is doing it."

— *St. Augustine*

June 3 ───────────────── *Heaven*

"I have found Heaven on earth, since Heaven is God, and God is my soul."

— *St. Elizabeth of the Trinity*

June 4 ───────────────── *Humility*

"Not every quiet man is humble, but every humble man is quiet."

— *St. Isaac the Syrian*

June 5 —————————— *Good Works*

"I am not capable of doing big things, but I want to do everything, even the smallest things, for the greater glory of God."

– St. Dominic Savio

June 6 —————————— *Trusting God*

"I knew God would take care of all and make everything right in the end."

– St. Mary MacKillop

June 7 —————————— *Gossip*

"There is no need to pay attention to gossip, much less get ill by giving in to those who perhaps have never known what truth is."

– Bl. Pier Giorgio Frassati

June 8 —————————— *Kindness*

"You will accomplish more by kind words and a courteous manner than by anger or sharp rebuke, which should never be used except in necessity."

– St. Angela Merici

June 9 ————————————— *Perseverance*

"Most Holy Sacred Heart of Jesus, help my heart to persevere in all that is holy."

– St. Rita of Cascia

June 10 ————————————— *Spiritual Riches*

"Let us become like Christ, since Christ became like us. He assumed the worse that He might give us the better; He became poor that we through His poverty might be rich."

– St. Gregory of Nazianzen

June 11 ————————————— *Death*

"It is a loving act to show sadness when our dear ones are torn from us, but it is a holy act to be joyful through hope and trust in the promises of God."

– St. Paulinus of Nola

June 12 ————————————— *Education*

"All battles are first won or lost, in the mind."

– St. Joan of Arc

June 13 ———————————————— *Love*

"Love the poor tenderly, regarding them as your masters and yourselves as their servants."

– St. John of God

June 14 ———————————— *God's Creation*

"Every day, my love for the mountains grows more and more. If my studies permitted, I'd spend whole days in the mountains contemplating the Creator's greatness in that pure air."

– Bl. Pier Giorgio Frassati

June 15 ———————————— *Sanctification*

"Prayer, good reading, the frequentation of the sacraments, with the proper dispositions, and particularly the flight of idleness – these are, believe me, the means of sanctifying yourself."

– St. Paul of the Cross

June 16 ———————————————— *Generosity*

"I do not lend. I give. Hasn't the good God been the first to give to me?"

– St. John Vianney

June 17 —————————— *Evangelization*

"We must teach more by example than by word."
> – *St. Mary MacKillop*

June 18 —————————— *Penance*

"It is impossible to find a saint who did not take prayer and penance seriously."
> – *St. Francis Xavier*

June 19 —————————— *Friendship*

"For in this way especially does a friend differ from a flatterer: The flatterer speaks to give pleasure, but the friend refrains from nothing, even that which causes pain."
> – *St. Basil the Great*

June 20 —————————— *Desolation*

"In times of desolation, God conceals Himself from us so that we can discover for ourselves what we are without Him."
> – *St. Margaret of Cortona*

June 21 ———————————————— *Prayer*

"It is better to say one Our Father fervently and devoutly than a thousand with no devotion and full of distraction."
— *St. Edmund*

June 22 ———————————————— *Suffering*

"Don't look for sufferings, but do not refuse them. Value them as precious marks of favor that He bestows on you."
— *Bl. Sebastian Valfre*

June 23 ———————————————— *Faith*

"I believe though I do not comprehend, and I hold by faith what I cannot grasp with the mind."
— *St. Bernard of Clairvaux*

June 24 ———————————————— *Happiness*

"My children, the three acts of faith, hope, and charity contain all the happiness of man upon earth."
— *St. John Vianney*

June 25 ——————————— *Forgiveness*

"Not the power to remember, but its very opposite, the power to forget, is a necessary condition for our existence."

– St. Basil the Great

June 26 ——————————— *The Eucharist*

"The surest, easiest, shortest way is the Eucharist"

– St. Pope Pius X

June 27 ——————————— *Temptation*

"Do not grieve over the temptations you suffer. When the Lord intends to bestow a particular virtue on us, He often permits us first to be tempted by the opposite vice. Therefore, look upon every temptation as an invitation to grow in a particular virtue and a promise by God that you will be successful, if only you stand fast."

– St. Philip Neri

June 28 ——————————— *Perfection*

"True perfection consists in having but one fear: the fear of losing God's friendship."

– St. Gregory of Nyssa

June 29 ——————— *The Our Father*

"When you say the Our Father, God's ear is next to your lips."

– St. Andre Besette

June 30 ——————— *Faith*

"You will never be happy if your happiness depends on getting solely what you want. Change the focus, get a new center, will what God wills, and your joy no man shall take from you."

– Bl. Fulton Sheen

JULY

July 1 ———————— *Pleasing God*

"Don't think that pleasing God lies so much in doing a great deal as in doing it with good will, without possessiveness and the approval of men."

– St. John of the Cross

July 2 ———————— *Love*

"We find rest in those we love, and provide a resting place to those who love us."

– St. Bernard of Clairvaux

July 3 ———————— *Health*

"It is not the soul alone that should be healthy; if the mind is healthy in a healthy body, all will be healthy and much better prepared to give God greater service."

– St. Ignatius of Loyola

July 4 ———————— *Prayer*

"There is nothing the devil fears so much, or so much tries to hinder, as prayer."

– St. Philip Neri

July 5 ——————————— *Eternity*

"How can you admire the heavens, my son, when you see that you are more permanent than they? For the heavens pass away, but you will abide for all eternity with Him forever."

– St. Gregory of Nyssa

July 6 ——————————— *Secret Giving*

"God is more pleased by one work, however small, done secretly, without desire that it be known, than a thousand done with desire that men know of them."

– St. John of the Cross

July 7 ——————————— *Evangelization*

"If I can succeed in saving only a single soul, I can be sure that my own will be saved."

– St. Dominic Savio

July 8 ——————————— *Regrets*

"Regret not that which is past; and trust not to thine own righteousness."

– St. Anthony of Padua

July 9 ———————————————— *Eternity*

"We must often draw the comparison between time and eternity. This is the remedy of all our troubles. How small will the present moment appear when we enter that great ocean."

– St. Elizabeth Ann Seton

July 10 ———————————————— *Love*

"We become what we love and who we love shapes what we become."

– St. Clare of Assisi

July 11 ———————————— *Love of Neighbor*

"Our life and our death is with our neighbor. If we gain our brother, we have gained God, but if we scandalize our brother, we have sinned against Christ."

– St. Anthony the Great

July 12 ———————————————— *Friendship*

"True friendship ought never to conceal what it thinks."

– St. Jerome

July 13 ———————————— *Society*

"Truly, matters in the world are in a bad state; but if you and I begin in earnest to reform ourselves, a really good beginning will have been made."

– St. Peter of Alcantara

July 14 ———————————— *Modesty*

"The dress of the body should not discredit the good of the soul."

– St. Cyprian of Carthage

July 15 ———————————— *Order*

"Where there is order, there is also harmony; where there is harmony, there is also correct timing; where there is correct timing, there is also advantage."

– St. Irenaeus

July 16 ———————————— *Study*

"Let devotion accompany all your studies, and study less to make yourself learned than to become a saint. Consult God more than your books, and ask Him, with humility, to make you understand what you read."

– St. Vincent Ferrer

July 17 _____ *Treasure*

"A Christian's treasure is not on earth. It is in heaven. Well, then! Our thoughts must go where our treasure is. Man has a fine function: to pray and to love. You pray, you love: that is man's happiness on earth!"

– *St. John Vianney*

July 18 _____ *Social Justice*

"Wherever people are suffering, wherever they are humiliated by poverty or injustice, and wherever a mockery is made of their rights, make it your task to serve them."

– *St. John Paul the Great*

July 19 _____ *Spiritual Warfare*

"Faith means battles; if there are no contests, it is because there are none who desire to contend."

– *St. Ambrose of Milan*

July 20 _____ *Suffering*

"The more we are afflicted in this world, the greater is our assurance in the next; the more we sorrow in the present, the greater will be our joy in the future."

– *St. Isidore*

July 21 _____ *Failure*

"Every fall, even if it be very grave and repeated, serves us always and only as a little step towards a higher perfection.
— *St. Maximilian Kolbe*

July 22 _____ *Books*

"Books are the most wonderful friends in the world. When you meet them and pick them up, they are always ready to give you a few ideas. When you put them down, they never get mad; when you take them up again, they seem to enrich you all the more."
— *Bl. Fulton Sheen*

July 23 _____ *Our Crosses in Life*

"Apart from the cross, there is no other ladder by which we may get to heaven."
— *St. Rose of Lima*

July 24 ———————————— *Prayer*

"Fasting is the soul of prayer, mercy is the lifeblood of fasting. So if you pray, fast; if you fast, show mercy; if you want your petition to be heard, hear the petition of others. If you do not close your ear to others, you open God's ear to yourself."

– St. Peter Chrysologus

July 25 ———————————— *Holy Scripture*

"All who ask receive, those who seek find, and to those who knock it shall be opened. Therefore, let us knock at the beautiful garden of Scripture. It is fragrant, sweet, and blooming with various sounds of spiritual and divinely inspired birds. They sing all around our ears, capture our hearts, comfort the mourners, pacify the angry, and fill us with everlasting joy."

– St. John of Damascus

July 26 ———————————— *Purity*

"Do you know that often a root has split a rock when allowed to remain in it? Give no place to the seed of evil, seeing that it will break up your faith."

– St. Cyril of Jerusalem

July 27 ——————— *Spiritual Reading*

"You will not see anyone who is truly striving after his spiritual advancement who is not given to spiritual reading."

– St. Athanasius

July 28 ——————— *Thanksgiving*

"The secret of happiness is to live moment by moment and to thank God for all that He, in His goodness, sends to us day after day."

– St. Gianna Molla

July 29 ——————— *Fear*

"I fear nothing, because of the promises of Heaven; for I have cast myself into the hands of Almighty God, who reigns everywhere."

– St. Patrick

July 30 ——————— *Love*

"The proof of love is in the works. Where love exists, it works great things. But when it ceases to act, it ceases to exist."

– St. Pope Gregory the Great

July 31 _____ *Trusting God*

"Put yourself in God's hands; He abandons no one."

— *St. Andre Bessette*

AUGUST

August 1 _____ *Faith*

"Don't be anxious about what you have, but about what you are."

— *St. Pope Gregory the Great*

August 2 _____ *God's Wisdom*

"I knew nothing; I was nothing. For this reason God picked me out."

— *St. Catherine Laboure*

August 3 _____ *Salvation*

"The Lord is loving unto man, and swift to pardon, but slow to punish. Let no man therefore despair of his own salvation."

— *St. Cyril of Jerusalem*

August 4 _____ *Remembering God*

"Remember God more often than you breathe."

— *St. Gregory of Nazianzen*

August 5 ——————————— *Troubles*

"Do not let your troubles disturb your trust in God."

– St. Mary MacKillop

August 6 ——————————— *Generosity*

"If you wish to help someone, give secretly and avoid arrogance."

– St. Ephrem

August 7 ——————————— *God's Love*

"If we love Jesus, we shall be loved in return by Him, and that is perfect happiness."

– St. Rose Philippine Duchesne

August 8 ——————————— *Critics*

"Nothing would be done at all, if a man waited until he could do it so well that no one could find fault with it."

– St. John Henry Newman

August 9 ——————————————— *Mercy*

"By your prayers you can bring down the rain of mercy."
— *St. Charbel Makhlouf*

August 10 ——————————————— *Trusting God*

"The best thing for us is not what we consider best, but what the Lord wants of us."
— *St. Josephine Bakhita*

August 11 ——————————————— *Hope*

"Do not lose heart, even if you should discover that you lack qualities necessary for the work to which you are called. He who called you will not desert you, but the moment you are in need he will stretch out his saving hand."
— *St. Angela Merici*

August 12 _____ *Parenting*

"Isn't it absurd to send children out to jobs and to school, and to do all you can to prepare them for these, and yet not to 'bring them upon in the chastening and admonition of the Lord (Eph. 6:4)?' Discipline is needed, not eloquence; character, not cleverness; deeds, not words. These gain a man the kingdom."

– St. John Chrysostom

August 13 _____ *Anxiety*

"Anxiety is the greatest evil that can befall a soul except sin. God commands you to pray, but He forbids you to worry."

– St. Francis de Sales

August 14 _____ *Young People*

"The principal trap that the devil sets for young people is idleness. This is a fatal source of all evil. Don't let there be any doubt in your mind that man is born to work, and when he doesn't do so, he's out of his element and in great danger of offending God."

– St. John Bosco

August 15 ———————— *Teaching*

"To touch the hearts of your students is the greatest miracle you can perform."

– St. John Baptist de La Salle

August 16 ———————— *Planning*

"As to the past let us entrust it to God's mercy, the future to Divine Providence. Our task is to live holy the present moment."

– St. Gianna Molla

August 17 ———————— *Childhood*

"Be a good child, and God will help you."

– St. Joan of Arc

August 18 ———————— *Spiritual Warfare*

"Arm yourself with prayer rather than a sword; wear humility rather than fine clothes."

– St. Dominic

August 19 ———————————— *Love of Neighbor*

Quote: "Let us learn to feel for the ills our neighbors suffer, and we will learn to endure the ills they inflict."
— St. John Chrysostom

August 20 ———————————— *Discipline*

"It is impossible for our human nature ever to stop moving; it has been made by its Creator ever to keep changing. Hence when we prevent it from using up its energy on trifles, and keep it on all sides from doing what it should not, it must necessarily move in a straight path towards truth."
– St. Gregory of Nyssa

August 21 ———————————— *Trusting God*

"Whoever does not trust the Lord in small matters is quite clearly an unbeliever in things of greater importance."
– St. Basil the Great

August 22 ———————————— *Sickness*

"Every illness and every trial is permitted by God as the means whereby we can best ensure our salvation."
– Bl. Sebastian Valfre

August 23 —————————— *Harsh Words*

"See to it that you refrain from harsh words. But if you do speak them, do not be ashamed to apply the remedy from the same lips, that inflicted the wounds."

– St. Francis of Paola

August 24 —————————— *Failure*

"When we are conscious of having failed and done wrong, we must humble ourselves before God, implore his pardon, and then quietly move ahead. Our defects should make us humble, but never cowardly."

– St. Clement Mary Hofbauer

August 25 —————————— *Our Crosses in Life*

"Do as the merchant does with his merchandise: Make a profit on every item. Don't allow the loss of the tiniest fragment of the true cross. It may be only the sting of a horsefly or the prick of a pin that annoys you; it may be a neighbor's little eccentricities, some unintended slight, the insignificant loss of a penny, some small restlessness of soul, a light pain in your limbs. Make a profit on every item as the grocer does, and you'll soon be wealthy in God."

– St. Louis de Montfort

August 26 _____ *Prayer*

"We must pray without tiring, for the salvation of mankind does not depend upon material success, but on Jesus alone."
> – *St. Frances Xavier Cabrini*

August 27 _____ *Sacrifice*

"The devil is afraid of us when we pray and make sacrifices. He is also afraid when we are humble and good. He is especially afraid when we love Jesus very much. He runs away when we make the Sign of the Cross."
> – *St. Anthony of Padua*

August 28 _____ *Charity*

"Charity is that with which no man is lost, and without which no man is saved."
> – *St. Robert Bellarmine*

August 29 _____ *Thanksgiving*

"Thank God ahead of time."
> – *Bl. Solanus Casey*

August 30 ———————— *Serving God*

"I want to live as He wishes and I want to serve Him as He likes, and nothing more."

— *St. Rose Venerini*

August 31 ———————— *Courage*

"The good Lord does not do things by halves; He always gives what we need. Let us then carry on bravely."

— *St. Zelie Martin*

SEPTEMBER

September 1 ———————— *Belief*

"All things are possible for him who believes, more to him who hopes, even more to him who loves."

— St. Lawrence of Brindisi

September 2 ———————— *God's Love*

"Nothing is far from God."

— St. Monica

September 3 ———————— *Life*

"Fear not that thy life shall come to an end, but rather fear that it shall never have a beginning."

— St. John Henry Newman

September 4 ———————— *Patience*

"It is patience that reveals every grace to you, and it is through patience that the saints received all that was promised to them."

— St. Pachomius the Great

September 5 _____ *Truth*

"Proclaim the truth and do not be silent through fear."
– St. Catherine Of Siena

September 6 _____ *Gossip*

"If something uncharitable is said in your presence, either speak in favor of the absent, or withdraw, or if possible stop the conversation."

– St. John Vianney

September 7 _____ *Troubles*

"Lay all your cares about the future trustingly in God's hands, and let yourself be guided by the Lord just like a little child."

– St. Edith Stein

September 8 _____ *Holy Fear*

"I am not afraid. I was born to do this."

– St. Joan of Arc

September 9 ——————————— *Mercy*

"Speak to them of the great mercy of God. Sometimes people are helped by your telling of your own lamentable past."

– St. Francis Xavier

September 10 ——————————— *Devotion*

"Love Him totally, who gave Himself totally for your love."
– St. Clare of Assisi

September 11 ——————————— *Trusting God*

"Trust God that you are exactly where you are meant to be."

– St. Teresa of Avila

September 12 ——————————— *Singing*

"And while we sing, remembering to sing is to doubly pray. At once in our hearts and our tongues, we offer double prayer sent heavenward on winged notes to praise God dwelling there."

– St. Cecilia

September 13 _____ *Mission*

"Lord, if your people need me, I will not refuse the work. Your will be done."

– St. Martin of Tours

September 14 _____ *Femininity*

"Both spiritual companionship and spiritual motherliness are not limited to the physical wife and mother relationship, but they extend to all people with whom woman comes into contact."

– St. Edith Stein

September 15 _____ *Life*

"Do not look back to the past, nor forward to the future. Claim only the present, for it holds God's will."

– St. Rose Philippine Duchesne

September 16 —————— *Compassion*

"Compassion, my dear Brother, is preferable to cleanliness. Reflect that with a little soap I can easily clean my bed covers, but even with a torrent of tears I would never wash from my soul the stain that my harshness toward the unfortunate would create."

- St. Martin de Porres

September 17 —————— *God's Creation*

"Every day that passes, I fall more desperately in love with the mountains... I am ever more determined to climb the mountains, to scale the mighty peaks, to feel that pure joy which can only be felt in the mountains."

– Bl. Pier Giorgio Frassati

September 18 —————— *Hardened Hearts*

"Pray to soften hardened hearts, to open darkened minds."

– St. Charbel Makhlouf

September 19 ———— *Loving Our Enemies*

"You don't love in your enemies what they are, but what you would have them to become."

– St. Augustine

September 20 ———————— *Fortitude*

"One of the duties of fortitude is to keep the weak from receiving injury; another, to check the wrong motions of our own souls; a third, both to disregard humiliations, and to do what is right with an even mind."

– St. Ambrose of Milan

September 21 ———— *The Least Among Us*

"When you have pity on the poor, you lend to God; and whoever gives to the least, gives to God–a sweet–smelling spiritual sacrifice to Him."

– St. Cyprian of Carthage

September 22 ———————— *Evangelization*

"I have never succeeded when I have spoken with the faintest suspicion of hardness. One must be ever on one's guard not to embitter the heart, if one wishes to move the mind."

– St. Vincent de Paul

September 23 ———————— *Suffering*

"Don't wince under the hammer that strikes you. Have an eye to the chisel that cuts you and to the hand that shapes you. The skillful and loving Architect may wish to make of you the chief stones of his eternal edifice and the fairest statues in his kingdom. Then let him do it. He loves you. He knows what he is doing. He has had experience. All his blows are skillful and straight and loving. He never misses, unless you cause him to by your impatience."

– St. Louis de Montfort

September 24 ———————— *God's Will*

"Never say to God: 'Enough!' Simply say: 'I am ready.'"

– Bl. Sebastian Valfre

September 25 ———————— *Praise*

"The most deadly poison of our times is indifference. And this happens, although the praise of God should know no limits. Let us strive, therefore, to praise Him to the greatest extent of our powers."

– St. Maximillian Kolbe

September 26 —————— *Almsgiving*

"Our prayers become effective through almsgiving; life is redeemed from dangers by almsgiving; souls are delivered from death by almsgiving."

– St. Cyprian of Carthage

September 27 —————— *Faith*

"If your faith were greater how much more peaceful you would be even when great trials surround and oppress you."

– St. Paula Frassinetti

September 28 —————— *Prayer*

"God is a spring of living water which flows unceasingly into the hearts of those who pray."

– St. Louis de Montfort

September 29 —————— *Compassion*

"We should love and feel compassion for those who oppose us, since they harm themselves and do us good, and adorn us with crowns of everlasting glory."

– St. Anthony Mary Zaccaria

September 30 ———————— *Priorities*

"Our business is to gain heaven, everything else is a sheer waste of time!"

— *St. Vincent de Paul*

OCTOBER

October 1 ———————— *God's Love*

"Cling to God and leave all the rest to Him. He will not let you perish. Your soul is very dear to Him. He wishes to save it."

– St. Margaret Mary Alacoque

October 2 ———————— *The Voice Within*

"Listen and attend with the ear of your heart."

– St. Benedict

October 3 ———————— *Work*

"Turn all your thoughts and aspirations to heaven. Work hard to secure for yourself a place there forever."

– St. Damian

October 4 ———————— *Speaking*

"Beware of much speaking, for it banishes from the soul the holy thoughts and recollection with God."

– St. Dorotheus

October 5 _____ *Reading*

"When we pray we speak to God; but when we read, God speaks to us."

— *St. Jerome*

October 6 _____ *Love of Neighbor*

"Those who are not good to others are bad to themselves."

— *St. Pope Leo the Great*

October 7 _____ *Justice*

"The rule of justice is plain: namely, that a good man ought not to swerve from the truth, nor inflict any unjust loss on anyone, nor act in any way deceitfully or fraudulently."

— *St. Ambrose of Milan*

October 8 _____ *Life of Faith*

"God is not satisfied with appearance. God wants the garment of justice. God wants his Christians dressed in love."

— *St. Oscar Romero*

October 9 _____ *Generosity*

"When we serve the poor and the sick, we serve Jesus. We must not fail to help our neighbors because in them we serve Jesus."

– St. Rose of Lima

October 10 _____ *Trusting in God*

"I trust in God and wish nothing else, but His will."

– St. Zygmunt Felinski

October 11 _____ *Evangelization*

"My job is to inform, not to convince."

– St. Bernadette Soubirious

October 12 _____ *Femininity*

"Being a wife and mother was never an obstacle to my spiritual life."

– Bl. Concepción Cabrera de Armida

October 13 _____ *Parenting*

"Depart, accursed fathers and mothers! Depart into the hell where the wrath of God awaits you, you and the good deeds you have done, while all the time you have let your children run wild. Depart into hell; they will not be long in joining you there."

– St. John Vianney

October 14 _____ *Continuous Learning*

"The saddest thing about any man, is that he be ignorant and the most exciting thing is that he knows it!"

– St. Alfred the Great

October 15 _____ *Saints*

"Ask Jesus to make you a saint. After all, only He can do that."

– St. Dominic Savio

October 16 _____ *Wisdom*

"I only seek in my old age to perfect that which I had not before thoroughly learned in my youth, because my sins were a hindrance to me."

– St. Patrick

October 17 ——————— *Total Surrender*

"Lean on your Beloved because the soul who abandons themselves in the hands of Jesus in all they do, is carried in his arms."

– St. Clare of Assisi

October 18 ——————— *Worry*

"There are no difficulties except for those who worry too much about tomorrow."

– St. Rose Philippine Duchesne

October 19 ——————— *Sports*

"Sports, balls, plays, festivities, pomps, are not in themselves evil, but rather indifferent matters, capable of being used for good or ill. I say that although it is lawful to amuse yourself, to dance, dress, feast, and see seemly plays—at the same time, if you are much addicted to these things, they will hinder your devotion, and become extremely hurtful and dangerous to you."

– St. Francis DeSales

October 20 _____ *Love*

"Love never says: I have done enough!"

         – *St. Marie Eugenie de Jesus*

October 21 _____ *The Word of God*

"Love is the most necessary of all virtues. Love in the person who preaches the word of God is like fire in a musket. If a person were to throw a bullet with his hands, he would hardly make a dent in anything; but if the person takes the same bullet and ignites some gunpowder behind it, it can kill. It is much the same with the word of God. If it is spoken by someone who is filled with the fire of charity–the fire of love of God and neighbor–it will work wonders."

         – *St. Anthony Mary Claret*

October 22 _____ *Doctrine and Good Works*

"God does not accept doctrines apart from good works, nor are works, when divorced from Godly doctrines, accepted by God."

         – *St. Cyril of Jerusalem*

October 23 ———————— *Prayer*

"Acquire the habit of speaking to God as if you were alone with Him, familiarly and confidence and love, as to the dearest and most loving of friends."

– St. Alphonsus Liguori

October 24 ———————— *Passions*

"A man who governs his passions is master of his world. We must either command them or be enslaved by them. It is better to be a hammer than an anvil."

– St. Dominic

October 25 ———————— *Thanksgiving*

"Be kindhearted to the poor, the unfortunate and the afflicted. Give them as much help and consolation as you can. Thank God for all the benefits he has bestowed upon you, that you may be worthy to receive greater."

– St. Louis IX

October 26 ——————— *Good Intention*

"If you are occupied during the whole meditation in fighting distractions and temptations you will have made a good meditation. The Lord looks to the good intention we have and the effort we make, and these He rewards."

– St. Francis de Sales

October 27 ——————— *Evangelization*

"Know that the greatest service that man can offer to God is to help convert souls."

– St. Rose of Lima

October 28 ——————— *Faith*

"The faith of those who live their faith is a serene faith. What you long for will be given you; what you love will be yours forever."

– St. Pope Leo the Great

October 29 ——————— *God's Timing*

"He loves, He hopes, He waits. Our Lord prefers to wait Himself for the sinner for years rather than keep us waiting an instant."

– St. Maria Goretti

October 30 ———————————— *Belief*

"I assure you that God is much better than you believe. He is content with a glance, a sigh of love."

— *St. Therese of Lisieux*

October 31 ———————————— *Death*

"When death cuts short a person's life, god immediately sends his angels to guard the soul on its return to its Creator."

— *St. Hugh of Lincoln*

NOVEMBER

November 1 ———————————— *Saints*

"Do not be afraid to be saints. Follow Jesus Christ who is the source of freedom and light. Be open to the Lord so that He may lighten all your ways."

– St. John Paul the Great

November 2 ———————————— *Sorrow*

"Sorrow can be alleviated by good sleep, a bath, and a glass of wine."

– St. Thomas Aquinas

November 3 ———————————— *Faith*

"He did not say: You will not be troubled–You will not be tempted–You will not be distressed. But He said: You will not be overcome."

– St. Julian of Norwich

November 4 ———————————— *Compassion*

"The Lord has loved me so much: we must love everyone. We must be compassionate."

– St. Josephine Bakhita

November 5 ———————————— *Life*

"The past is no longer yours; the future is not yet in your power. You have only the present wherein to do good."

– St. Alphonsus Liguori

November 6 ———————————— *Hope*

"If you do not hope, you will not find what is beyond your hopes."

– St. Clement of Alexandria

November 7 ———————————— *Books*

"Let books be your dining table, and you shall be full of delights."

– St. Ephrem

November 8 ———————— *God's Abundance*

"There is nothing we can desire or want that we do not find in God."

– St. Catherine of Siena

November 9 _____ *Humility*

"The first degree of humility is prompt obedience."

– St. Benedict

November 10 _____ *Humility*

"Humility is the virtue that requires the greatest amount of effort."

– St. Rose Philippine Duchesne

November 11 _____ *Friendship*

"Friendship is the source of the greatest pleasures, and without friends even the most agreeable pursuits become tedious."

- St. Thomas Aquinas

November 12 _____ *Excellence*

"No one can ever excel in great things who do not first excel in small things."

– St. Francis Xavier

November 13 _____ *Cussing*

"Filthy talk makes us feel comfortable with filthy action. But the one who knows how to control the tongue is prepared to resist the attacks of lust."

– St. Pope Clement I

November 14 _____ *Exercise*

"Remember that bodily exercise, when it is well ordered, as I have said, is also prayer by means of which you can please God our Lord."

– St. Ignatius of Loyola

November 15 _____ *God's Creation*

"For when one considers the universe, can anyone be so simple-minded as not to believe that the Divine is present in everything, pervading, embracing and penetrating it?"

– St. Gregory of Nyssa

November 16 ——————— *Evangelization*

"If you truly want to help the soul of your neighbor, you should approach God first with all your heart. Ask him simply to fill you with charity, the greatest of all virtues; with it you can accomplish what you desire."

— St. Vincent Ferrer

November 17 ——————— *Motherhood*

"To be a mother is to nourish and protect true humanity and bring it to development."

— St. Edith Stein

November 18 ——————— *Timidity*

"The greatest obstacle in the apostolate of the Church is the timidity or rather the cowardice of the faithful."

— St. Pope Pius X

November 19 ——————— *Solitude*

"Settle yourself in solitude, and you will come upon God in yourself."

— St. Teresa of Avila

November 20 _____ *Prayer*

"We must pray without ceasing, in every occurrence and employment of our lives—that prayer which is rather a habit of lifting up the heart to God as in a constant communication with Him."

– St. Elizabeth Ann Seton

November 21 _____ *Confession*

"Confession heals, confession justifies, confession grants pardon of sin, all hope consists in confession; in confession there is a chance for mercy."

– St. Isidore

November 22 _____ *Our Crosses in Life*

"The cross is the way to paradise, but only when it is borne willingly."

– St. Paul of the Cross

November 23 _____ *Fasting*

"When a man begins to fast, he straightway yearns in his mind to enter into conversation with God."

– St. Isaac the Syrian

November 24 ———————————— *Faith*

"It is good that faith should precede reason, lest we seem to demand reasons from our Lord God in the same way that we might demand them of a man. How unworthy it would be to believe the human testimonies of another, and not believe the utterances of God Himself!

– St. Ambrose of Milan

November 25 ———————————— *Hope*

"Those whose hearts are enlarged by confidence in God run swiftly on the path of perfection. They not only run, they fly; because, having placed all their hope in the Lord, they are no longer weak as they once were. They become strong with the strength of God, which is given to all who put their trust in Him."

– St. Alphonsus Liguori

November 26 ———————————— *Peace*

"Without any doubt there is a desire in all hearts for peace. But how foolish is he who seeks this peace apart from God; for if God be driven out, justice is banished, and once justice fails, all hope of peace is lost."

– St. Pope Pius X

November 27 _____ *Peace*

"Who except God can give you peace? Has the world ever been able to satisfy the heart?"

– St. Gerard Majella

November 28 _____ *Prayer*

"Prayer is the root, the fountain, the mother of a thousand blessings."

– St. John Chrysostom

November 29 _____ *Trusting God*

"Act, and God will act."

– St. Joan of Arc

November 30 ___ *Becoming All We Can Be*

"Jesus, help me to simplify my life by learning what you want me to be–and becoming that person."

– St. Therese of Lisieux

DECEMBER

December 1 _____ *God's Love*

"We are not the sum of our weaknesses and failures, we are the sum of the Father's love for us and our real capacity to become the image of His Son Jesus."

– St. John Paul the Great

December 2 _____ *Faith*

"If God can work through me, he can work through anyone."

– St. Francis of Assisi

December 3 _____ *Total Surrender*

"There is a state of resting in God; an absolute break from all intellectual activity, when one forms no plans, makes no decisions, and for the first time really ceased to act; when one simply hands over the future to God's will and 'surrenders himself to Fate.'"

– St. Benedicta of the Cross

December 4 _____ *Love*

"First let a little love find entrance into their hearts, and the rest will follow."

– St. Philip Neri

December 5 ————————— *Kindness*

"No act of kindness, no matter how small, is ever wasted."

– St. Sebastian

December 6 ————————— *Charity*

"True charity consists in doing good to those who do us evil, and in thus winning them over."

– St. Alphonsus Liguori

December 7 ————————— *Good Works*

"A single act of pure love pleases Me more than a thousand imperfect prayers."

– St. Faustina (from a vision of Jesus)

December 8 ————————— *Reverence*

"Be a Catholic: When you kneel before an altar, do it in such a way that others may be able to recognize that you know before whom you kneel."

– St. Maximilian Kolbe

December 9 ———————— *Paradise*

"One earns paradise with one's daily tasks."
— *St. Gianna Molla*

December 10 ———————— *Grace*

"God can no more withhold His grace from a soul pre-pared to receive it than the sun can fail to shine through an open window."
— *St. John Fisher*

December 11 ———————— *Social Justice*

"The ones who have a voice must speak for those who are voiceless."
— *St. Oscar Romero*

December 12 ———————— *Friendship*

"True friendship can harbor no suspicion; a friend must speak to a friend as freely as to his second self."
— *St. Jerome*

December 13 —————— *Moderation*

"The more a man uses moderation in his life, the more he is at peace, for he is not full of cares for many things."

– St. Anthony the Great

December 14 —————— *Femininity*

"Since Mary is the prototype of pure womanhood, the imitation of Mary must be the goal of girls' education."

– St. Edith Stein

December 15 —————— *Possibilities*

"Consult not your fears but your hopes and your dreams. Think not about your frustrations, but about your unfulfilled potential. Concern yourself not with what you tried and failed in, but with what it is still possible for you to do."

– St. Pope John XXIII

December 16 ———— *Material Possessions*

"The rich man is not one who is in possession of much, but one who gives much."

– St. John Chrysostom

December 17 _____ *Mary*

"Let Mary never be far from your lips and from your heart. Following her, you will never lose your way. Praying to her, you will never sink into despair. Contemplating her, you will never go wrong."

– St. Bartholomew

December 18 _____ *Family Life*

"The family is the basis in the Lord's plan, and all the forces of evil aim to demolish it. Uphold your families and guard them against the grudges of the evil one by the presence of God."

– St. Charbel

December 19 _____ *Life*

"Life is a succession of moments; to live each one is to succeed."

– St. Dymphna

December 20 _____ *Charity*

"Charity wins souls and draws them to virtue."

– St. Angela Merici

December 21 _____ *Generosity*

"Reflect that in reality you have a greater need to serve the poor than they have of your service."

– St. Angela Merici

December 22 _____ *Prayer*

"There is no danger if our prayer is without words or reflection because the good success of prayer depends neither on words nor on study. It depends upon the simple raising of our minds to God, and the more simple and stripped of feeling it is, the surer it is."

– St. Jane Frances de Chantal

December 23 _____ *Good Works*

"A tree is known by its fruit; a man by his deeds. A good deed is never lost; he who sows courtesy reaps friendship, and he who plants kindness gathers love."

– St. Basil the Great

December 24 _____ *Secret Faith*

"The most beautiful act of faith is the one made in darkness, in sacrifice, and with extreme effort."

– St. Padre Pio

December 25 ———————— *Generosity*

"Give something, however small, to the one in need. For it is not small to one who has nothing. Neither is it small to God, if we have given what we could."

– St. Gregory Nazianzen

December 26 ———————— *The Saints*

"The saints must be honored as friends of Christ and children and heirs of God. Let us carefully observe the manner of life of all the apostles, martyrs, ascetics, and just men who announced the coming of the Lord. And let us emulate their faith, charity, hope, zeal, life, patience under suffering, and perseverance unto death so that we may also share their crowns of glory."

– St. John of Damascus

December 27 ———————— *Reading*

"Only God knows the good that can come about by reading one good Catholic book."

– St. John Bosco

December 28 _____ *Silence*

"He who can keep silence is near to God."

– Bl. Sebastian Valfre

December 29 _____ *The Church*

"Christ has no body now on earth but yours, no hands, no feet but yours. Yours are the eyes with which Christ looks out his compassion to the world. Yours are the feet with which he is to go about doing good. Yours are the hands with which he is to bless us now."

– St. Teresa of Avila

December 30 _____ *God's Power*

"There is nothing impossible to God."

– St. Rita

December 31 _____ *Be the Light*

"A single sunbeam is enough to drive away many shadows."

– St. Francis of Assisi

Imagine how many

holy moments

you will trigger by introducing
this idea to six people!